I Wonder W

Stalactites Hang Down

and other questions about caves

Jackie Gaff

KING*f*ISHER

KINGFISHER

Kingfisher Publications Plc,
New Penderel House,
283-288 High Holborn,
London WC1V 7HZ
www.kingfisherpub.com

First published by Kingfisher Publications Plc 2003
First published in this format 2004
10 9 8 7 6 5 4 3 2 1

1TR/0204/SHE/UNV(RNB)/126.6MA(F)

A CIP catalogue record for this book is available
from the British Library

ISBN 0 7534 0952 6

Series designer: David West Children's Books
Author: Jackie Gaff
Consultant: Keith Lye
Illustrations: Peter Dennis 30l; Chris Forsey 8/9,
   24/25, 28/29; Mike Lacey (SGA) 4/5, 10/11,
   14/15, 26/27; Edward Mortelmans 31r;
   Nicki Palin 30/31m; Terry Riley (SGA) 18/19,
   20/21; Mike Taylor (SGA) 6/7, 12/13, 16/17,
   22/23; Peter Wilkes (SGA) all cartoons.

Printed in Taiwan

CONTENTS

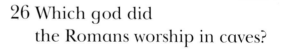

What is a cave?

A cave is a natural hollow or crack in the ground that's big enough for a large animal, such as a human, to pass inside. Sometimes a cave is a single, roomlike area called a chamber. In other places, several chambers are connected by passages. This is called a cave system.

Which is the biggest cave chamber?

The record-holder is the Sarawak Chamber in the Gunung Mulu National Park, in the Malaysian region of Sarawak, on the island of Borneo. It's a massive 700 metres long, 415 metres wide, and 80 metres high.

● With a depth of 1,710 metres, the Voronja (or Krubera) Cave in Georgia, east of the Black Sea, is the deepest cave to be explored so far.

Where is the longest cave system?

The US state of Kentucky is home to the world's longest-known cave system. It's called Mammoth Cave, and to date, explorers have mapped about 570 kilometres of passages. What's more, people think hundreds more kilometres may be waiting to be discovered!

● There's enough room inside the Sarawak Chamber to park 40 jumbo jets.

How do caves form?

Most caves form in a hard kind of rock called limestone as it is slowly dissolved, or eaten away, by acidic water. As rainwater falls through the air and down into the soil, it collects tiny amounts of carbon dioxide gas. This gas mixes with the rainwater to make a weak acid which is similar to the fizz in soft drinks. As the acidic water trickles down through tiny cracks, it slowly nibbles away the limestone and eventually carves out chambers and passages.

● Around 13 per cent of all rainwater ends up underground.

● Cave systems can contain streams, rivers and even lakes and waterfalls.

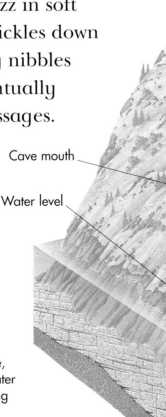

Cave mouth

Water level

● When streams or rivers flow through a cave, the sand and gravel carried by the rushing water may scrape at the rock like sandpaper, wearing the rock away and making the cave bigger.

● Vertical cave passages are called chimneys or potholes.

● A basin-like opening called a sinkhole may form on the surface if the roof of a cave collapses.

● Large horizontal passages are called galleries.

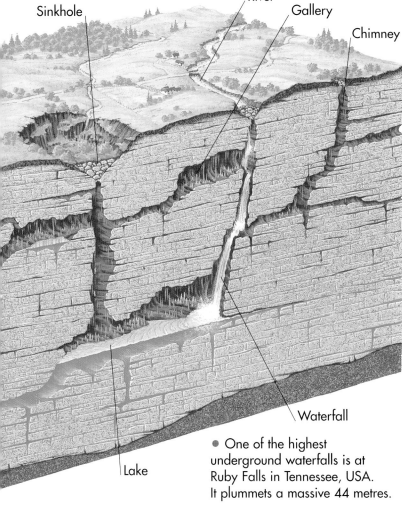

Sinkhole

River

Gallery

Chimney

Waterfall

Lake

● One of the highest underground waterfalls is at Ruby Falls in Tennessee, USA. It plummets a massive 44 metres.

What are stalactites and stalagmites?

Stalactites and stalagmites are spectacular, stony structures that sometimes form inside limestone caves. Both are roughly carrot-shaped, but while stalactites hold tight to the cave roof, mighty stalagmites are mounted on the cave floor.

● Stalactites and stalagmites can sometimes join up to make a column. One of the world's tallest is in Spain's Nerja Cave. It measures around 32 metres from top to bottom.

Stalagmite

Stalactite

Why do stalactites hang down?

As acidic water seeps downwards, it dissolves the mineral calcite which makes up most of the limestone. When this liquid drips and dribbles from a cave roof, some of the water evaporates and changes into a gas, leaving some of the minerals behind, as solids. Over time, these minerals may grow downwards to build stalactites.

- Stalactites never get to be as large as stalagmites. That's because when a stalactite gets very big, it becomes too heavy and crashes down from the cave roof.

Do you get fried eggs in caves?

You certainly do. Stalactites and stalagmites aren't the only amazing sights to be found in caves. Minerals can form all kinds of other weird and wonderful shapes and come in every shade of the rainbow. In the Luray Caverns, in the US state of Virginia, there are two mineral formations that look just like fried eggs!

Column

Flowstone

- Flowstone looks like a stone waterfall.

- Cave pearls can be the size of ping-pong balls.

Cave pearls

- Soda straws are hollow and look like the straws you sip drinks through. They are the beginning of a stalactite.

How do caves form inside icy glaciers?

A glacier is a huge, thick mass of ice that builds up in freezing cold places like the poles. But even in the world's chilliest spots, the weather usually heats up a little in summer. These warmer temperatures can make some of the ice inside a glacier melt and begin to flow away through cracks. In its turn, the warmer, flowing water can melt more and more ice, until it carves out a glacial cave.

● If a glacial cave isn't too deep below the surface, sunlight can filter down through the ice to fill the cave with an eerie blue glow.

● Some of the most stunning glacier caves are in Iceland, the land of ice and fire. Heat from volcanoes at the glaciers' lowest edges melts the ice, creating caves inside the glaciers.

Where is the 'World of the Ice Giants'?

You'll have to take a trip to Austria to visit the 'World of the Ice Giants', or *Eisriesenwelt*, the world's biggest system of ice caves. Unlike glacial caves, ice caves form inside solid rock, as a cave's rock walls become coated in ice that stays frozen all year round.

• In parts of the 'World of the Ice Giants', the ice is 20 metres thick.

What is a lava tube?

It is a cave formed by lava, the hot, runny rock that pours out when a volcano blows its top! Sometimes, when lava flows downhill, its outer layers cool and harden into a solid crust, but its inner layers stay runny. If this runny lava drains away, a tube-like cave is left behind.

How does the sea scoop out caves?

Sea caves form along rocky coastlines, as waves pound grit and pebbles against the land, and make holes in the cliffs. Sea caves are often well hidden, with tiny entrances that are difficult to find and even harder to get to. It's one reason why smugglers used to stash their booty inside them.

What is a blowhole?

Sometimes, wave power can bash a hole in a sea cave's roof. This is called a blowhole. When the seawater rises at high tide, waves pounding into the cave are squeezed upwards to squirt out of the blowhole like a huge fountain.

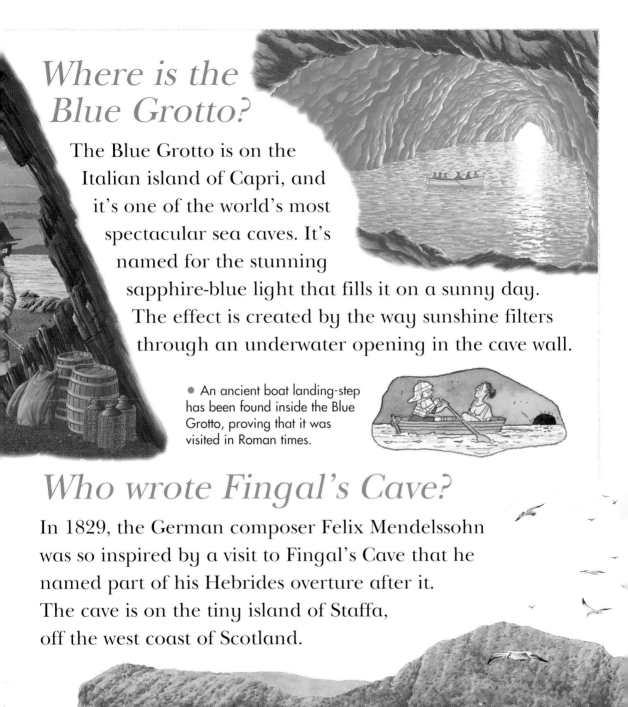

Where is the Blue Grotto?

The Blue Grotto is on the Italian island of Capri, and it's one of the world's most spectacular sea caves. It's named for the stunning sapphire-blue light that fills it on a sunny day. The effect is created by the way sunshine filters through an underwater opening in the cave wall.

● An ancient boat landing-step has been found inside the Blue Grotto, proving that it was visited in Roman times.

Who wrote Fingal's Cave?

In 1829, the German composer Felix Mendelssohn was so inspired by a visit to Fingal's Cave that he named part of his Hebrides overture after it. The cave is on the tiny island of Staffa, off the west coast of Scotland.

Where would you find a potholer?

Inside a cave, of course! Potholers are people who explore caves for sport. They are also known as cavers or spelunkers. Some potholers put on diving gear to explore flooded chambers and passages.

● Some cave passages are only just big enough for the potholer's body.

What is the first rule of potholing?

Never go inside a cave alone or without an experienced potholer as your guide. Potholers always explore in groups. Caves are very dangerous places, and only trained potholers have the knowledge, experience and equipment to explore them.

● Potholers protect themselves from jagged rocks by wearing helmets, and heavy-duty clothing and shoes. They carry ropes and other climbing gear to help them climb up and down rock shafts.

Why do potholers wear a lamp on their heads?

The deeper you go inside a cave, the darker, damper and colder it gets. Potholers need lamps to help them find their way. Their lamps are on their helmets so their hands are free to help them climb, or crawl and wriggle through narrow cave passages.

Where is the twilight zone?

A cave is a mini-world of different light and temperature zones, with various animals visiting or making their homes throughout. Some sunlight and rainfall reaches the entrance zone, and the temperature there is similar to that outside. The twilight zone is darker, damper and cooler. The dark zone of the inner cave is even cooler and wetter, and it's always pitch-black.

● The entrance zone – birds such as cliff and cave swallows may build nests on rocky ledges here, while insects and other creatures scuttle about on the cave floor.

Can plants survive in caves?

You sometimes find shade-loving plants such as ferns and mosses growing near the entrance to a cave, but green plants can't survive the darkness of the twilight and dark zones.

● All living things need water, and even animals can't survive in the depths of a dry cave.

- The twilight zone – bats love to shelter here, as do snakes, some kinds of cave salamander and all sorts of cave minibeasts.

- The dark zone – the pools, lakes and rivers of this zone are home to strange, ghostly, pale kinds of cave fish, cave crayfish and cave shrimps.

- Many different animals may live in a cave. For instance, scientists have found more than 200 kinds in the USA's Mammoth Cave in Kentucky.

Do mushrooms grow in caves?

Yes, they do. Mushrooms aren't plants, but a kind of fungi, and fungi love the cool, damp, dark conditions inside caves. Bacteria, or germs, are another non-plant life-form that can survive away from the light.

Do deer live in Deer Cave?

No, deer prefer woodland to caves. Despite its name, Deer Cave in Sarawak's Gunung Mulu National Park is famous for its bats – around five million of them! Bats are night animals, and they love caves because they love the dark. They spend the daylight hours dozing upside down from the cave roof. When dusk falls, they wake and fly outside to hunt for their dinner.

● The record for the biggest bat colony is thought to belong to Bracken Cave, in the US state of Texas. As many as 20 million Mexican free-tailed bats spend part of the year there.

● Around 200,000 bats per minute stream out of Deer Cave at dusk!

How do bats hunt in the dark?

Although most bats have fairly good eyesight, this doesn't help them much at night. Instead of relying on their eyes, bats also use their ears. Each bat sends out a stream of high-pitched squeaks, then listens to the echoes made by the sounds bouncing back off rocks, insects and other objects. This technique is called echo-location, and it helps bats find their way, and track food such as moths, in the dark.

● Some bats have a fold of skin called a nose-leaf on their snout. Scientists think that the nose-leaf can be used to aim echo-location squeaks that help pinpoint a tasty target.

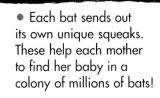

● Each bat sends out its own unique squeaks. These help each mother to find her baby in a colony of millions of bats!

Which cave bird's nest is turned into soup?

Bird's-nest soup is a Chinese delicacy – a food that is much prized in the East. It's made from the nests of swiftlets, a kind of bird that lives in caves and uses echo-location. Instead of building their nests from twigs, the swiftlets weave them from their saliva, or spit, which cements the twigs to the cave wall.

● The nests are chewy but fairly tasteless, so flavourings such as chicken stock are used to liven up the soup.

● Prying the swiftlets' nests from the cave wall is one of the world's most dangerous jobs. Collectors climb incredible heights up bamboo poles to reach them.

Why do oilbirds go click-clack?

Oilbirds also live in caves and use echo-location to find their way around in the darkness.

But unlike a bat's echo-location sounds, which are usually far too high for our ears to hear, an oilbird's are lower. An oilbird's echo-location noise sounds like the click-clack of an old-fashioned typewriter!

Do bears live in caves?

● In North America, other cave guests include pack rats, raccoons and wildcats.

Bears will take shelter from cold winter weather if they come across a cosy cave, but they don't live in caves all year round. Like bats and birds, bears are cave guests, not cave dwellers.

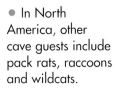

● A cave dweller is an animal that spends its entire life inside a cave. A cave guest is an animal that visits a cave for part of the year, to shelter or hunt for food.

Which cave is lit by insects?

There's no need to take a torch when you visit the magical Glowworm Grotto in New Zealand's Waitomo Cave. Its roof is lit by thousands of tiny glowworms that sparkle and twinkle like tiny, blue fairy-lights.

● The famous New Zealand opera singer, Kiri Te Kanawa, once gave a concert in another part of the Waitomo Cave, called the Cathedral.

Why are cave fish blind?

These fish are cave dwellers, and like other creatures that spend their whole lives deep underground, they don't need sight because they live in total darkness. Instead of sight, cave fish have special nerve endings in their skin which help them 'feel' their way about and track down food.

Cave fish

Which insects feed on bat droppings?

Bat droppings, or guano, are a rich source of food for cave minibeasts such as cockroaches, flies and millipedes. In their turn, these creatures are snapped up by centipedes, crickets and spiders, which are then hunted by larger cave animals such as bats and birds.

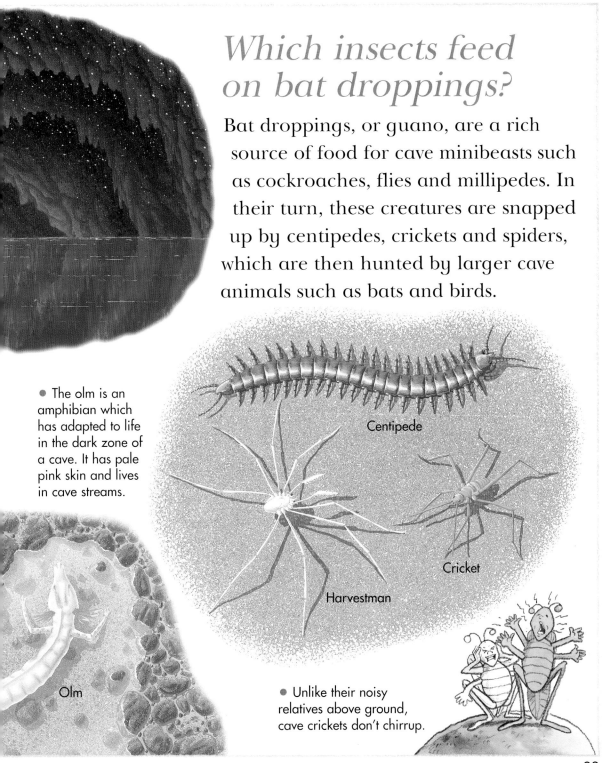

- The olm is an amphibian which has adapted to life in the dark zone of a cave. It has pale pink skin and lives in cave streams.

Centipede

Harvestman

Cricket

Olm

- Unlike their noisy relatives above ground, cave crickets don't chirrup.

What are the Lascaux Cave treasures?

Inside the Lascaux Cave in southwestern France there are ancient treasures that are far more precious than piles of glittering gold. The cave walls are covered with hundreds of lifelike paintings and carvings of animals – charging bulls, bison, musk-ox, galloping horses and leaping reindeer. The age of these magnificent pictures is even more astonishing – prehistoric artists began creating them around 17,000 years ago.

● The cave artists' yellow, red and brown paint came from kinds of earth called ochre, while white came from clay or chalky stones. Black came from the charcoal of burnt wood.

● Lascaux was discovered in 1940, by four boys on a walk. One story tells how they found their way into the cave by trying to rescue their dog after it fell down a hole.

● Cave artists painted with their fingers, or with brushes made by fixing animal fur to sticks. Sometimes they blew paint through hollow bones – an early kind of spray-painting!

● Some of the images on the Lascaux walls are of animals that have long since become extinct and vanished from the earth – for example, mammoths and cave bears.

Who buried their dead in caves?

The ancient Egyptians are famous for building vast pyramids, but there was a big drawback to these huge above-ground tombs. Every robber in the land could see exactly where the dead person's mummy and its treasures were buried. By about 3,500 years ago, theft was such a problem that the Egyptians came up with a new idea. They began to carve secret cave-tombs into the rock, where their dead could be hidden away from the robbers' thieving fingers.

● The walls of the cave-tombs were decorated with beautiful paintings, many of them illustrating everyday life in ancient Egyptian times.

Which god did the Romans worship in caves?

One of the most important gods for Roman soldiers was Mithras, the god of light, who was portrayed slaying a bull in a cave. For this reason, soldiers worshipped Mithras in cave-temples they dug out underground.

What are the catacombs?

The ancient Egyptians weren't the only people to bury their dead in caves. Catacombs are cave-tombs that Jews and early Christians began digging into soft rock beneath the city of Rome nearly 2,000 years ago.

● The Maraca people lived in Brazil, South America, more than 400 years ago. They made human-shaped urns from clay to hold the bodies of their dead, and used natural caves as holy places to store the urns.

Where is the rose-red city in the rock?

● One of Petra's most magnificent buildings is a 40-metre high temple called the Khazneh.

Some ancient peoples carved out entire cities underground or inside hills. Among the most famous is Petra, in what is now Jordan. It is called the rose-red city because of the rich colour of its rock.

Do people live in caves today?

Yes, they do – either in natural caves, or in rooms they've dug out of the rock. In the Shanxi Province of northern China, for instance, millions of people live in cave homes. Some families even grow crops on their roofs.

● It's so hot during the summer that almost all buildings in the Australian mining town of Coober Pedy are underground. The town is a centre for opal mining, and around 2,500 people live there.

Where can you play sport in a cave?

In Norway's Gjøvik Rock Cavern, which was blasted from the rock to house a huge underground sports stadium where ice-hockey matches were held during the 1994 Winter Olympics. At 91 metres long and 61 metres wide, it's one of the world's largest artificial rock chambers.

● Saumur, in France's Loire Valley, is also famous for its cave homes. The caves were dug out in the 18th century by stonemasons, who used the stone to build the valley's great chateaux.

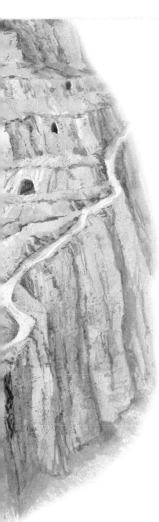

Why are caves good for cheese?

Caves are the key to one of France's tastiest cheeses – Roquefort. It is made from sheep's milk, and its special flavour comes from the streaks of blue-coloured mould. Moulds are fungi, like mushrooms, and they grow from seeds called spores. These are added to the sheep's milk in the early stages. The young cheeses are put in a network of caves, which provide the right climate for the spores to grow into mould.

● Cave conditions are also ideal for storing wine and for farming all kinds of edible mushroom.

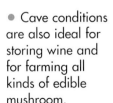

Which sun goddess hid in a cave?

When the Japanese sun goddess Amaterasu hid in a cave, the whole world was plunged into darkness. Nothing would persuade her out until Uzume, the goddess of laughter, began to dance outside the cave. When Amaterasu sneaked a look, she was so fascinated by her own reflection in a magical mirror that she came out, restoring light to the world forever.

● The Zuni people of the southwestern USA believed that the first men and women were strange-looking creatures who came from four caves in the underworld. When they first came out of the caves, the god Yanauluha taught them how to grow plants and to survive above ground.

● The Maya people of South America believed in a cave-dwelling bat god called Zotz, who had the body of a human, but the head and wings of a bat.

What is a troll?

In Viking and other Scandinavian legends, trolls are scary creatures, much bigger and stronger than humans. They live in caves, only leaving them after dark to hunt for their favourite dinner – humans!

● In ancient Greek legends, a cyclops was a one-eyed giant who lived in caves and ate raw flesh, including that of humans.

Index